T 599 759 HAR

KILLER CATS

CHEETAHS

By R. P. Harasymiw

Gareth Stevens
Publishing

Please visit our website, www.garethstevens.com. For a free color catalog of all our high-quality books, call toll free 1-800-542-2595 or fax 1-877-542-2596.

Library of Congress Cataloging-in-Publication Data

Harasymiw, R. P.
Cheetahs / R.P. Harasymiw.
   p. cm. — (Killer cats)
Includes index.
ISBN 978-1-4339-7000-9 (pbk.)
ISBN 978-1-4339-7001-6 (6-pack)
ISBN 978-1-4339-6999-7 (library binding)
1. Cheetah—Juvenile literature. I. Title.
QL737.C23H3558 2012
599.75'9—dc23
                   2011043885

First Edition

Published in 2013 by
Gareth Stevens Publishing
111 East 14th Street, Suite 349
New York, NY 10003

Copyright © 2013 Gareth Stevens Publishing

Designer: Daniel Hosek
Editor: Therese Shea

Photo credits: Cover, p. 1 Masterfile.com; all background images, pp. 9, 11, 13, 15, 19, 21 Shutterstock.com; p. 5 Jupiter Images/Getty Images; p. 6 (paw inset) Martin Harvey/Peter Arnold/Getty Images; pp. 6–7 Taxi/ Getty Images; p. 17 Anup Shah/Thinkstock.com.

Contents

Boldface words appear in the glossary.

On the Run

Imagine sitting in a car speeding down a highway. Suddenly, a large spotted cat races by! Though this is unlikely to happen to you, it's possible for a cheetah to run faster than a car. In fact, a cheetah may run as fast as 70 miles (113 km) an hour! This big cat is the fastest land animal on Earth.

The cheetah's speed makes it a deadly cat. Once a cheetah spots its **prey**, it only needs a few seconds to catch its meal.

Cheetahs are found in some African countries and in the Middle Eastern country of Iran.

Built for Speed

Cheetahs look like speedy animals. They have long legs and thin bodies. A cheetah's claws are always out. They dig into the ground and push the cheetah's body forward. The cheetah's backbone, or spine, bends to help it change direction quickly.

The cheetah has a tail as long as 31.5 inches (80 cm). Its tail gives the cheetah balance. It also works somewhat like the **rudder** of a boat. When a cheetah changes direction, its tail helps it turn!

THAT'S WILD!

The cheetah is the only cat with claws that don't pull back into its paws.

6

A cheetah's body
may be 4.5 feet
(1.4 m) long.

7

Looking for Dinner

Cheetahs can live in many kinds of **habitats**, including open grasslands, bushy plains, and mountains. They just want to be near food! Cheetahs eat small and medium-size animals, such as **antelope**, hares, and baby **wildebeest**.

Cheetahs have good eyesight so they can spot an animal from far away. Sometimes they sit in trees so they can see even better. A cheetah has black marks called tear tracks that run from the inside corner of each eye to its mouth. Some people think tear tracks help keep sunlight out of a cheetah's eyes.

THAT'S WILD!

Cheetahs can go from 0 to 60 miles (97 km) per hour in 3 seconds.

A cheetah's large heart and big lungs help it reach high speeds.

9

The Chase

When a cheetah sees its prey, it creeps closer. The cheetah's coloring and spotted coat make it hard to see in tall, dry grass. Cheetahs need to be near their prey when they begin to move.

When the cheetah is close enough, it races at top speed and trips or knocks down its prey. Though cheetahs are fast, they can't run at top speed for very long. Most chases last less than a minute. Then the cheetah bites the animal's neck to kill it.

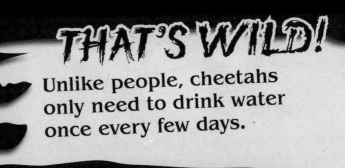

THAT'S WILD!

Unlike people, cheetahs only need to drink water once every few days.

Cheetahs give up easily if they don't catch their prey on the first try. Only half of all cheetah hunts are successful.

Fast Food

After a cheetah catches its prey, it's very tired. It can take up to a half hour to catch its breath before it can eat. However, the cheetah needs to eat quickly or other animals—such as lions, **hyenas**, and vultures—will steal its meal.

A cheetah is a good runner but not a good fighter. It can't fight the animals that want its prey. So the cheetah often drags its kill to a hidden place so it can rest and eat.

THAT'S WILD!

A cheetah's **stride** is as long as 25 feet (7.6 m) when it's running. At its fastest, it makes three strides per second.

Unlike many cats, cheetahs are more active during the day than at night.

13

Cheetah Cubs

Some cheetahs live alone, while others live in small groups. Males and females come together to **mate** but don't spend much time together otherwise. A mother cheetah may have as many as six cubs at a time.

Cheetah cubs are born with their eyes closed. They don't have teeth until they're 3 weeks old. Their mother moves them to a new den every few days to keep them safe. In some places, only about one out of every ten cheetah cubs lives through the first 6 weeks.

This cheetah cub already has long, sharp teeth. It's ready to learn to hunt. ▶

Growing Up Cheetah

At first, a mother cheetah leaves her cubs behind when she hunts. After about 6 weeks, the cubs follow her. They start to "play hunt" with each other and chase animals. Sometimes, the mother catches a live animal and brings it back to her cubs so they can try to kill it.

After about a year and a half, the mother cheetah leaves her cubs. Cheetah brothers may stay together their entire lives. They're often chased away from their sisters by other male cheetahs.

THAT'S WILD!

Cheetahs that live in a group make chirping noises to each other.

Cheetah cubs are born with grayish fur. This helps keep them hidden in tall, dark grass.

17

In Danger!

Cheetahs once lived in Asia, North America, and Europe. Today, they live in Africa and Iran. There are only about 10,000 cheetahs left in the wild.

The biggest danger to cheetahs is people. People take their land to build and farm. Farmers kill cheetahs to keep their livestock safe.

In recent years, people have been trying to help cheetahs. Farmers use dogs to scare cheetahs away instead of killing them. Special areas have been set aside where cheetahs can't be hunted.

Cheetahs have been on Earth longer than any other big cat.

Cheetahs don't roar like lions. However, they purr, hiss, and growl.

19

An Honored Animal

Cheetahs were once honored in many places. Egyptian rulers kept them as pets. An ancient Indian ruler is said to have had 1,000 cheetahs! People trained cheetahs for hunting games. Many statues and paintings of cheetahs from thousands of years ago still exist.

More must be done to help these big cats. Cheetahs in zoos don't have babies often. Cheetahs must be allowed to roam and have families in their wild habitats or they'll disappear forever.

long legs

large heart and lungs

long tail

CHEETAHS
Born to Run

bendable spine

thin body

claws always out

Glossary

antelope: an animal somewhat like a deer that is found in Africa and Asia

habitat: an area where plants, animals, and other living things live

hyena: a dog-like animal found in Africa and Asia

mate: to come together to make babies

prey: an animal that is hunted by other animals for food

rudder: an underwater blade that is used to direct a boat

stride: a long step

wildebeest: a large antelope with a head like an ox

For More Information

BOOKS

Clarke, Ginjer L. *Cheetah Cubs*. New York, NY: Grosset & Dunlap, 2007.

Eckart, Edana. *Cheetah*. New York, NY: Children's Press, 2005.

Silverman, Buffy. *Can You Tell a Cheetah from a Leopard?* Minneapolis, MN: Lerner, 2012.

WEBSITES

Cheetahs
kids.nationalgeographic.com/kids/animals/creaturefeature/cheetah/
Find many fun facts and photos as well as a video on this site.

What Makes a Cheetah Run So Fast?
animals.howstuffworks.com/mammals/cheetah-speed.htm
Learn the keys to a cheetah's speed and much more.

Index